NIGHT SKY
STORIES

FOLLOW THE
DRINKING
GOURD

AN UNDERGROUND RAILROAD STORY

A RETELLING BY
CARI MEISTER

ILLUSTRATED BY
ROBERT SQUIER

PICTURE WINDOW BOOKS
a capstone imprint

Follow the Drinking Gourd is an American folk song. The song explains how slaves in the southern United States could follow the Big Dipper and the North Star to freedom in the North.

Before the Civil War (1861–1865), many slaves escaped and made their way north using stars to guide them. Historians are unsure if a man named Peg Leg Joe went from plantation to plantation singing *Follow the Drinking Gourd*. But there was a system of people and places called the Underground Railroad. They helped slaves on the run by giving them safe places to stay along the way.

Peg Leg Joe was a traveling man. He enjoyed hot muggy nights walking down dirt roads. He enjoyed meeting new people. But most of all, he loved to sing. His favorite song was *Follow the Drinking Gourd*. He loved this song because it was a secret map that helped slaves in the South find freedom in the North.

Peg Leg Joe worked as he traveled from plantation to plantation in the South. Sometimes he built shelters. Sometimes he worked in the fields. But at night around the campfire, Joe sang *Follow the Drinking Gourd* to the slaves.

"Listen closely," Joe said. "This song is a map to freedom."

When the sun comes back,
And the first quail calls,
Follow the drinking gourd.
The old man is awaiting for to carry you to freedom
If you follow the drinking gourd.

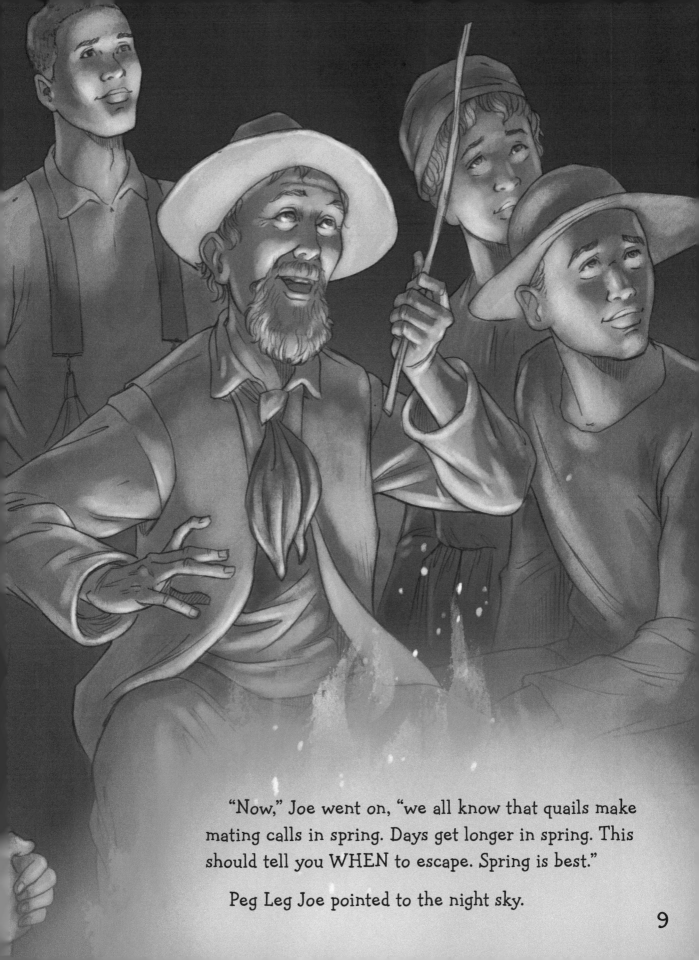

"Now," Joe went on, "we all know that quails make mating calls in spring. Days get longer in spring. This should tell you WHEN to escape. Spring is best."

Peg Leg Joe pointed to the night sky.

Follow the drinking gourd,
Follow the drinking gourd,
The old man is awaiting for to carry you to freedom
If you follow the drinking gourd.

"See that big dipper in the sky?" Joe asked.
"That's the drinking gourd. See that really big bright
star directly above it? That star always points north."

The slaves knew what north meant—freedom!

The river bank will make a mighty good road
The dead trees show you the way
Left foot, peg foot, traveling on
Follow the drinking gourd.

"Listen up," Joe said. "This is important. The first river in the song is the Tombigbee River. Follow that waterway. The water will help hide your scent. Slave catchers and their dogs can't track you in water."

Joe picked up a stick. He drew in the dirt and said, "I marked dead trees on the path like this."

He made a picture of a left footprint next to a circle. He tapped his wooden leg and chuckled. "The circle is my peg leg!"

The river ends between two hills,
Follow the drinking gourd,
There's another river on the other side,
Follow the drinking gourd.

"When the Tombigbee River ends," Joe said, "you will see a mountain. From a distance it looks like two hills. The river starting there is the Tennessee River. Stick to the left side of that river—it points north."

15

Peg Leg Joe knew this was a lot of information to remember. So he quizzed the people about what the words meant.

"Who is the old man?" Joe asked.

"He's you?" a child said.

"He's a preacher," one woman answered.

"I know," a man said, "he's a Quaker."

Joe smiled. "All of you are right! There will be many helpers along the way."

"The rivers in this part of the song are the Ohio River and the Tennessee River. The two rivers meet in Paducah, Kentucky. Paducah is near Kentucky's border with Illinois."

"Do you know what is in Illinois?" Peg Leg Joe asked.

At this point, it got quiet around the campfire. Faces glowed. Some people laughed. Some cried. But they all whispered the same thing, "Freedom."

LEARN MORE

Thousands of people in the southern United States escaped slavery using the Underground Railroad. Unlike the song says, the best time to escape was late fall. The slaves on the run could steal food from the fields. Fall also brought more darkness, which was better for hiding.

The journey was dangerous. Some people on the run were caught. Others died along the way. But many people did make it to freedom.

GLOSSARY

Civil War—(1861–1865) the battle between states in the North and South that led to the end of slavery in the United States

plantation—a large farm or estate where many workers are needed to help with the crops

preacher—a leader of a church

Quaker—a highly religious person; Quakers often helped slaves escape

slavery—the owning of other people; slaves are forced to work without pay

Underground Railroad—a large system of people and places that helped slaves escape to freedom

Editor's Note: In 1928 the Texas Folklore Society first published *Follow the Drinking Gourd*. Lee Hays also published a version of the song in 1947. We have used Hays' lyrics in this book.

READ MORE

Levine, Ellen. *Henry's Freedom Box.*
New York: Scholastic Press, 2007.

Mortensen, Lori. *Harriet Tubman:*
Hero of the Underground Railroad.
Biographies. Minneapolis: Picture
Window Books, 2007.

Rey, H. A. *Find the Constellations.*
Boston: Houghton Mifflin Harcourt, 2008.

INTERNET SITES

FactHound offers a safe, fun way to find
Internet sites related to this book. All
of the sites on FactHound have been
researched by our staff.

Here's all you do:

Visit *www.facthound.com*

Type in this code: 9781404873759

Super-cool stuff!

Check out projects, games and lots more at
www.capstonekids.com

LOOK FOR ALL THE BOOKS IN
THE NIGHT SKY STORIES SERIES:

FOLLOW THE
DRINKING GOURD

THE STORY OF **CASSIOPEIA**

THE STORY OF **ORION**

THE STORY OF **URSA MAJOR**
AND **URSA MINOR**

Thanks to our advisers for their expertise, research,
and advice:
Richard Cooper, Interpretive Services Manager
National Underground Railroad Freedom Center, Cincinnati

Terry Flaherty, PhD, Professor of English
Minnesota State University, Mankato

Editor: Shelly Lyons
Designer: Alison Thiele
Art Director: Nathan Gassman
Production Specialist: Danielle Ceminsky
The illustrations in this book were created digitally.

Picture Window Books
1710 Roe Crest Drive
North Mankato, Minnesota 56003
877-845-8392
www.capstonepub.com

Library of Congress Cataloging-in-Publication Data
Meister, Cari.
Follow the drinking gourd : an Underground Railroad
story / a retelling by Cari Meister ; illustrations by
Robert Squier.
    p. cm. — (Night sky stories)
Summary: Peg Leg Joe travels from plantation to plantation
singing the Drinking Gourd song that will guide slaves to
freedom in the North.
ISBN 978-1-4048-7375-9 (library binding)
ISBN 978-1-4048-7714-6 (paperback)
ISBN 978-1-4048-7987-4 (ebook PDF)
1. Underground Railroad—Juvenile fiction. 2. Slavery—
Juvenile fiction. 3. African Americans—Juvenile fiction.
4. Songs—Juvenile fiction. [1. Underground Railroad—
Fiction. 2. Slavery—Fiction. 3. African Americans—Fiction.
4. Songs—Fiction.] I. Squier, Robert, ill. II. Title.
 PZ7.M515916Fol 2013
 813.6—dc23   2012000904